YOU CAN OVERCOME BY THE BLOOD OF JESUS

3RD EDITION

Written by

DR KINGSLEY OTURU
(MBBS, PHD)

ENTERING INTO YOUR DIVINE
DOMINION
YOU CAN OVERCOME BY THE BLOOD
3RD EDITION

DEDICATION

This book is dedicated to my parents Bishop. Dr. and Mrs. O. M. Oturu for their positive impact in my life, their unfailing love and encouragement.

COPYRIGHT

ACKNOWLEDGEMENTS

I would like to thank the LORD God Almighty for His grace and faith in writing this book. I appreciate Jesus for saving me and the Holy Spirit for His inspiration and strength even in times of discouragement and trials.

This book is not the work of one person. I will like to express my sincere gratitude to the many people who have been of great help in seeing this book published.

I appreciate Pastor and Pastor Mrs. Dele Bamgboye (High Flyers Church) for reading through and suggestions on the original manuscript. I must appreciate Pastor Benny Hinn for his insightful teachings and revelations on the Holy Spirit. I also appreciate Pastor Larry Mauriello (World Healing Fellowship/Benny Hinn Institute) for his kind support. Special appreciation to Bishop Francis and Pst. Margaret Boampong (Intercessory Ministry of Great Britain) for wonderful support and prayers. I appreciate Prof. Raphael and Doris Mrode and the African Caribbean Christian Fellowship Family. I appreciate Eng. Wole and Blessing Obawole and Emeka and Ifeoma Offor.

Special thanks Bishop David Oyedepo whose teachings on divine favour and faith have radically transformed my life. I also appreciate Winners Chapel for life changing messages.

I appreciate Glory Oturu. I appreciate my son Joshua Oturu for his playful distractions. I appreciate my parents Bishop and Rev. Mrs. Kate Oturu for their love and support. I am thankful to my siblings, Chris, Nkiru, Dave and Alex. I am grateful to Sylvia

Eneke, Enoma Ifueko, Dr Olumide Ogundegi, Dr Chimezie Isikiakau, Dr Tari Iyalla, Dr Okorie Uloma, Dr S. Fatoki and Rita. God bless Gloria Azubuike m cousin as well. Uncles Gabriel Azubuike, Adol Okebugwu and Ngozi Anyogu and their families are also appreciated

I am grateful to Mrs E. Adimorah, Nigeria Christian Corpers fellowship Rivers state, Alex Etim, Ifeoma Dan Nwude, Pst Wisdom, Pst Kemi Adesola, Anna Modi, Stella Otuh, Ntachiobi Okuwa, Maria Arshad, Prof. Winifred Ijomah, Prof Wale Coker, Dr Achi Chibueze and everyone who in one or the other has helped to see that the publishing of this book is a success.

TABLE OF CONTENT

DEDICATION...III

COPYRIGHT I

ACKNOWLEDGEMENTS II

TABLE OF CONTENT...IV

INTRODUCTION.. 1

CHAPTER 1 JESUS OUR REDEEMER 5

CHAPTER 2 ALL POWER BELONGS TO JESUS 10

CHAPTER 3 A NEW COVENANT..............................16

CHAPTER 4 YOU CAN BE MADE RICH BY THE BLOOD........22

CHAPTER 5 OVERCOMING POWER IN THE BLOOD 27

CHAPTER 6 PRAYING WITH THE BLOOD...........................36

CHAPTER 7 THE HOLY COMMUNION 43

CHAPTER 8 THE HEALING POWER IN THE BLOOD 47

ABOUT THE AUTHOR 55

INTRODUCTION

A s I write this book on the blood of Jesus with awe, I know it is power packed with the blessings of God, as the fire of God burns in my heart.

The blood is the life-giving essence of man. The Word of God says, "The life of the flesh is in the blood" (Lev. 17:11). Without adequate amount of blood in the body, one is said to have anaemia or pancytopenia, medically. Unless blood is transfused or haematinics (blood producing drugs) are administered, death is imminent. One going through the earth without contact with the Blood of Jesus amounts to risk of spiritual anaemia, death and destruction.

When Jesus rose up from the dead, he told his Disciples "Why do you look surprised". He asked, "Why do doubts arise in your hearts? See my hands ...a spirit does not have flesh and bone as you see that I have" (Luke 24:39). Notice that he said "I am flesh and bone" not flesh and blood. His blood had been shed and placed at a spiritual blood bank where believers would be able to draw from in times of need. We can overcome all of life's circumstances by the blood.

You'll be seeing true life experiences of believers overcoming by the blood. Isaac, Abraham's son was to be sacrificed him on the mountain of Moriah (Gen. 22:1-13) but relief came when a ram was slaughtered and blood sacrificed in exchange for Isaac by the Hand of God.

In Exodus 4:24, the Lord sought to kill Moses because of his doubt in the efficacy of God's word, but praise God, Zippora his wife had insight in the efficacy of the blood. Ex. 4: 25-26 records that she took a flint and cut off her son's foreskin and threw it at Moses' feet and said "You are indeed a bridegroom of blood to me" So He let him alone...because of the circumcision". When God saw the blood from the foreskin, He knew Zippora was moving into a higher frequency or a newer dimension, so He spared Moses life.

In Revelation 12:11, there was war in heaven, the angels of God were fighting against the demons of the devil. There was no breakthrough or deliverance until the angels pulled out that joker called "THE BLOOD". In card games, the joker is usually reserved at the background by wise players to be used as a last resort. The angels did just that and heaven records that "they overcame him because of the blood of the Lamb and the words of their testimony" (Rev. 12:8-11). The Blood rendered the devil and his cohorts powerless, impotent and weak.

"They were not strong enough and there was no longer a place found for them in heaven" (Rev. 12:8).

They lost their place in heaven because of the Blood. Thank God that He has risen us up together with Jesus and placed us in heavenly places far above principalities, powers, dominions and every other name that is named (Eph. 1:3). This therefore implies that sickness, plagues, scarcity, mediocrity and obscurity lose their place in your life because of the blood in Jesus Name.

The Blood settles all controversy. When two believers who have kept themselves pure, and ready for marriage meet for the first time as husband and wife, blood is shed as a sign of an everlasting covenant of love and mutual fidelity.

Pilate loved Jesus and tried to save him but the Jews cried "crucify him". Pilate washed his hands saying "I am innocent of this man's blood" (Matt. 27:24). He however had no choice but to meet the Jews' demand when they sheepishly answered, "His blood be on us and our children" (Matt 27:25), thus pronouncing a curse on themselves and their children. No wonder they have not been able to live in peace with the surrounding Arab countries despite all kinds of peace summits and negotiations. However, that curse can be turned into a blessing when they give their lives to Christ (John 3:16) as they were also inadvertently pleading the Blood of Jesus on themselves and their descendants.

Blood in the human body is used to provide nutrition and oxygen to the cells. They help fight bacteria and other microbes. However, if they become malignant or cancerous, they can cause damage and even death to the body. This is why blood covenants are very strong.

As we enter into the revelatory light of the power in the Blood, and you begin to apply the principles highlighted, you can be rest assured that obstacles in your life will be transformed into miracles and every setback will be used to set you up in Jesus' name. Jesus was pierced in His hands with blood flowing so that your hands will not suffer lack. When Jesus died on the cross, as His Blood contacted the earth, the curtains of the temple tore and the earth quaked. As His Blood contacts your life, every form of negativity and adversity will be torn to pieces and you will enter into a realm of peace in Jesus' name.

CHAPTER 1
JESUS OUR REDEEMER

T wap! Twap! Twap! The sparrows perching on the nearby tree flutter away as the "Twapping" of the throng held in the hands of a Roman soldier, reached for Jesus' back. Repeatedly the whip flung through the air, striking Jesus' body violently on the orders of Pontius Pilate (Jn. 19:1). A throng of a scourge is an instrument of torture or punishment usually reserved for criminals. It is a whip composed of a handle to which is tied three of more lashes of leather or cords. Occasionally some sharp bones are connected to its end to help draw blood from the victim's back.

Pain, agony and anguish perused through Jesus' body as the whip struck His back. Dissatisfied with their torture, the soldiers weave a crown of thorns and squash it on Jesus' head causing Blood to drip from his scalp. The soldiers spit on Him and use a tall hard weed called a reed to repeatedly hit Him on the head. Jesus could have easily released himself and commanded platoon of angels to destroy the blasphemers. However, He didn't because of His love for mankind. It was the Father's good please for all the fullness to dwell in Him.

"And through Him to reconcile all things to himself, having made peace through the blood of His cross" (Col. 1:20).

Jesus passed through all the grief, ache and sorrow so as to deliver mankind from the wiles of the devil. He is given a heavy wooden cross to carry. Slowly, insidiously but irrefutably He struggles to carry the cross to the hill of Golgotha (which interpreted means the place of the skull). Golgotha was the execution ground for criminals in Jesus' days. Exhaustion, hunger and dehydration take their toll on him. So fatigued is He that Simon from Cyrene is forced by the soldiers to help Jesus, carry His cross (Mark 15:21).

At last Jesus is crucified between two thieves. In a voice of triumph, He cries, "It is finished" (Jn. 19:30). He then bows His head and gives up His Spirit. The devil thought that he had won a mighty victory. He did not realise that this was God's master plan to deliver mankind from the hands of the devil. Jesus had to trust that God the Father would not forsake Him but would be with Him to raise Him up from the dead.

"I glorified Thee on the earth, having accomplished the work, which thou hast given Me to do. And now glorify Thou me together with Thyself, Father, with the glory, which I had with Thee before the world was" (Jn. 17:4-5).

Jesus went into the very pits of Hell to purchase man back from the bondage of the devil. Adam, the first man created by God had delivered mankind into the hands of the devil together with the earth and all that God had placed in man's hands (Luke 4:6). The Psalmist saw this in the spirit and prophesied.

"Lift up your heads oh ye gates and be thou lifted up o ye everlasting doors that the King of Glory may come in. Who is this king of Glory ....The Lord strong and mighty He is the king of Glory. (Psalm 24:7-10)."

Jesus went into the camp of the enemy and pulverized his camp I like the way the Bible puts it.

"Having spoilt principalities and powers He made an open show (a public display) of them having triumphed over them through Him." (Cor. 2:15).

Jesus seized the keys of hell and death wherewith the devil had held man captive and declared *"All power has been given to me in heaven and on earth" (Matt 28:18).* Yes! Jesus has freed man from the bondage of the devil. I pray the bondage of sin sickness and failure is destroyed from your life in Jesus' name Because Jesus humbled Himself to the extent of dying on the cross, God has now highly exalted Him and given Him a name that is above every principality, power, throne, dominion and every other name that is named. Not only in this world but in the world to come (Phil 2:9).

At the name of Jesus, every knee has to bow and every tongue will confess that he is Lord (Phil 2:10). Jesus is now highly exalted and guess what? We as believers who have been washed by the blood of Jesus are also lifted up together with Jesus, so that we are seated together with Him in the heavenly realm far above all demonic principalities and powers (Eph 2:6). Perhaps as you are reading this book, you feel depressed and frustrated Life has not been dealing fairly with. you. You stumble from one problem to another. Your finances are in shambles. You don't know where you next pay check is going to come from. Maybe your friends have deserted you and you simply don't have peace in your heart.

Perhaps someone you thought loved you has broken your heart. The Prince of Peace; Jesus is able to give you peace in your heart and take care of all your problems. All you need to do is to tell Him to come into your life and take absolute control. You've been trying different techniques in life and have ended up in failure.

Why not try Jesus? You have absolutely nothing to lose but everything to gain. If you want to make Jesus the Lord of your life; you want to be lifted up with Him in the heavenly places and say no to the devil and sin so that Heaven can become your home simply say this prayer from your heart and you will be saved. For with the heart man believes unto righteousness and with the mouth, confession is made unto salvation (Rom 10:10).

Jesus is standing at the door of your heart and knocking. If you open up, He'll come into your heart and cause a radical transformation. Start studying God's word the Bible and join a Bible believing full gospel church and your life will be positively changed in Jesus Name:

"Heavenly Father, I realize that without you, I am a sinner and that I cannot help myself. I believe that you sent your Son Jesus Christ to die for my sins and that He arose on the third day for my justification. I hereby renounce every covenant I might have made with the devil or that might have been made on behalf, by my parents, relatives or friends. I confess all my sins and claim the cleansing and reconciling power in the blood of Jesus. Jesus please kindly come into my life. I receive Jesus into my heart as my LORD and Saviour. Fill me and Transform

my life with your Spirit and grant me the grace to live according to your will and purpose in Jesus' name, Amen."

CHAPTER 2
ALL POWER BELONGS TO JESUS

A s Jesus hung on the cross, He gave up His spirit, which went up to the heavenly realm to purchase back what the devil had stolen from man. The Bible says in Matt. 4:8,

"Again, the devil took Him to a very high mountain and showed him all the kingdoms of the world and their glory; and he said to Him 'all these things will I give you if you fall down and worship me".

Jesus did not argue with the devil as the enemy had taken over power of the kingdoms of the earth from man. Having paid the price of redemption, Jesus proceeded to the pits of hell to take back the rightful place of man and to sit on His throne as King of kings and the Lord of lords. I like the way Philippians 2:8-10 puts it.

"And being found in appearance as a man, He humbled Himself by becoming obedient to the point of death, wherefore God hath exalted Him and given Him a name above every other name that at the name of Jesus, every knee shall bow and every tongue confess that Jesus is Lord".

The devil could not contend with the blood of Jesus, as Jesus pulverized the enemy and his cohorts. Col. 2:15 says that when he had spoilt (disgraced, disarmed) principalities and powers (i.e. rulers and authorities in hell), he made the public show of the forces of darkness having triumphed over them. When you are affiliated to Jesus, He links you back to the power God gave to man before he tasted the forbidden fruit.

Hence, Jesus says: "I will give you the keys of the Kingdom of heaven, and whatever you bind on earth shall be bound in heaven, and whatever you shall loose on earth shall be loosed in heaven" (Matt 16:19; 18:18).

Jesus has taken the keys back and is ready to give you access if you take hold of is blood. Jesus is the 'tree of life' that was in the Garden of Eden. As many as eat of Him shall never perish but have everlasting life. Remember God "stationed the cherubim (a terrible angel) and the flaming sword which turned in every direction to guard the way of the tree of life (Gen. 3:24). So, if the tree of life is in you (i.e. Jesus) the cherubim have been stationed to guard you from the wiles of the devil. No weapon formed against you shall prosper in Jesus Name.

HOW MAN FELL

To fully grasp what Jesus did on the cross we need to go back to the Garden of Eden to see how man fell from the position that God had placed him. Man was created in the image and the likeness of God. God placed man in control of the whole earth and all that was in it. He gave man charge over the birds, fish and all the other animals on earth. Adam was to take control of every creeping thing on the earth (Gen. 1:26). Man was to subdue the earth and take total authority (Gen. 1:28).

The devil (angel of darkness, the enemy) however came into the Garden of Eden and caused man to disobey God. He tricked man into losing his dominion on the earth. The devil has not always been an angel of transgression but actually served God in heaven as an angel of light.

"You had the seal of perfection Full of wisdom and perfect in beauty. You were in Eden, the garden of God; every precious stone was your covering; the ruby the topaz and the diamond; the beryl the onyx and the jasper; the lapis lazuli, the turquoise, and the emerald; and the gold, the workmanship of your settings and the sockets, was in you. On the day that you were created they were prepared. You were the anointed cherub who covers, and I placed you there. You were on the holy mountain of God; you walked in the midst of the stones of fire. You were blameless in your ways from the day you were created" (Ezekiel 28:12-15).

The devil however became proud and stirred up a revolt against God.

"Your heart was lifted up because of your beauty; you corrupted your wisdom by reason of your splendor (Ezekiel. 28:17).

He caused a rebellion and together with some other angels (demons), tried to take over the kingdom of God. However, he failed woefully.

"How you have fallen from heaven, O star of the morning, son of dawn! You have been cut down to the earth you have weakened the nations! But you said in your heart, 'I will ascend to heaven; I will raise my throne above stars for God and I will sit on the mount of assembly in the recesses of the north.'" (Is. 14:12-13).

He wanted to be like God. God dealt with him and threw him down to the earth, waiting for his final judgment in hell. The devil did not want to go down alone and so hatched a plan to get man entangled in sin. The devil caused man to fall for the same sin that struck him out of heaven and cut him down to the earth; pride. God wanted a family of people that would worship Him and take control of the earth. He thus created man.

"Let us make man in Our image according to our likeness; and let them rule over the fish of the sea and over the birds of the sky and over the cattle and over all the earth, and over every creeping thing that creeps on the earth (Genesis 1:26).

God placed the first man, Adam in control of the Garden of Eden and indeed the whole earth including the devil. He gave him the ministry of dressing and keeping the earth.

"And God blessed them; and said to them be fruitful and multiply and fill the earth and subdue it; and rule over the fish of the sea and over the birds of the sky and over every living thing that moves on the earth" (Gen. 1:28).

He also gave Adam a mate and a helper/companion in his wife (Eve). God however gave them a command that they could eat of any of the animals or fruits of the trees on the earth, but that of the tree of 'knowledge of good and evil' in the midst of the garden they were not to eat. (Gen. 2:16). The devil came to the woman in form of a serpent and said to her,

"Indeed, has God said, 'you shall not eat from every tree of the garden?" (Gen. 3:1).

Of course, God did not say that but the devil has always been a liar. God had told them that the day they eat the fruit they shall surely die. The devil lied and told her "You surely shall not die".

When the woman saw that the tree was good for food and that it was a delight to the eyes and desirable to make one wise, she took from its fruit and ate. She also gave to her husband and he did eat. (Gen. 3:6). Perhaps when man saw that she did not die physically, he doubted God's word and did eat the fruit. Unfortunately, the moment they ate the fruit they died spiritually, and put into motion the process for their physical death. Small wonder all kinds of diseases came into the human race. Man had brought in corruption through sin and brought the whole earth and the human race into damnation.

"So then as through one transgression there resulted condemnation to all men" (Rom. 5:18).

Hallelujah thank God that just as Adam brought condemnation to all mankind God now annulled this by sending His Son Jesus Christ to die for us. There is now therefore no condemnation unto those who are in Christ Jesus (Romans 8:1).

"So, through one act of righteousness, there resulted justification of life to all men. (Rom 5:18b).

God demonstrated His love for mankind by sending Jesus Christ to die for us while we were yet sinners. Jesus has saved as many as believe in Him from wrath. The Bible declares that all have sinned and fallen short of the glory of God (Rom 3:23). It also declares the wages of sin is death (i.e. eternal damnation in hell fire). Having faith in Jesus Christ brings you into the heavenly kingdom. If you belong to Christ then you are Abraham's offspring heirs according to promise. (Gal. 3:29).

Therefore, you are no longer a slave but a son and an heir through God. Through faith in Christ we can be connected to spiritual power that places us far above the devil problems of life and every work of darkness, not only in this world but also in the world to come. (Eph.1:20-21, 2:6). Hallelujah, we can take our rightful place of dominion on earth. Glory be to Almighty God.

CHAPTER 3
A NEW COVENANT

A covenant is an agreement between two or more people or between God and a person or group of people. In the spirit realm it is ratified with the shedding of blood. The first covenant God made with man is seen in Gen.9:8-18, when He promises never to destroy the earth with a flood. God even placed the rainbow in the sky to remind man of the covenant. God is seen making a covenant (The Abrahamic covenant) in Gen. 17:1-8, where He promises to bless him and all his descendants. As many as are linked to Jesus also partake of this covenant. In the old testament, the term "the covenant" usually refers to the covenant that God made with the Israelites at the time of Moses:

"And he sent young men of the sons of Israel, and they offered burnt offerings and sacrificed young bulls as peace offerings to the LORD. And Moses took half of the blood and put it in basins, and the other half of the blood he sprinkled on the altar. Then he took the book of the covenant and read it in the hearing of the people; and they said, "All that the LORD has spoken we will do, and we will be obedient!" So, Moses took the blood and sprinkled it on the people, and said, "Behold the blood of the covenant, which the LORD has made with you in accordance with all these words." (Ex. 24:5-8).

God had tried to bring man back to Himself through the Blood. As suggested earlier, the life of the flesh is in the blood (Lev. 17:11). As man had fallen and died spiritually, God prepared a new way to bring man back to Him. God is holy and just. He cannot condone or behold sin. However, when blood is shed, it covers sin and we can have fellowship with God. When Adam and Eve sinned against God, they were afraid and hid themselves, ashamed that they were naked. God performed the first sacrifice by killing an animal, shedding its blood and using its skin to cover them.

"And the LORD God made garments of skin for Adam and his wife, and clothed them" (Gen. 3:21).

There was atonement (at-one-ment) of sin by the blood. Man was made one with God by the blood. The blood of animals covered the sins of man. Hebrews 9:22 suggests that "without the shedding of blood, there is no remission of sins". Similarly, 1 John 1:7 confirms that Jesus' blood cleanses us from all sins.

"The life of the flesh is in the blood (lev.17:11)"

In the old covenant, when the children of Israel sinned, an animal was sacrificed and the blood of the animal was placed on the altar of God. The blood covered the sins of the children of Israel and God would forgive them of their sins. God however saw that the children of Israel still continued to sin. This meant that sacrifices had to be repeated every year.

"But in those sacrifices, there is reminder of sins year by year. For it is impossible for the blood of bulls and goats to take away sins" (Heb 10:4).

God hatched a plan to help not only the children of Israel', but the whole world to walk in holiness, and have their sins not just covered, but washed for good. There was a time I had a visitor come to our house. In a bid to arrange the house, some sauce fell and stained a white tablecloth. We found a napkin to cover the stain. Nobody noticed it, nevertheless it was still there. That's what the old covenant did. It covered our sins. Thank God for the blood of Jesus, this not just covers, but cleanses (i.e. bathes, washes, rinses and dips us clean). Because of Jesus, there is no need to sacrifice animals every year for our sins as the blood of Jesus was sacrificed once and for all.

"For by one offering, He has perfected for all time those who are sanctified" (Heb. 10:14).

Jesus saves forever those who come to Him by faith. He is in heaven praying and interceding on our behalf before our heavenly father whenever we fall astray.

"It is fitting that we should have such a high priest, holy, innocent, undefiled, separated from sinners and exalted above the heavens; who does not need daily, like those high priests to offer up sacrifices...because this He did once for all when He offered up Himself (Heb 7:26-27).

The first covenant with the children of Abraham was established with circumcision by the shedding of blood.

"This is my covenant, which you shall keep, between Me and you and your descendants after you; every male, child among you shall be circumcised" (Gen 17:10).

God made His covenant with Abraham with shedding of blood. This second covenant also needed to be ratified with the shedding of blood, with 'Jesus, the mediator of a new covenant and to the sprinkled blood, which speaks better than the blood of Abel' (Heb 12:24). As many as are in Christ are also blessed with Abraham. What's even more marvelous is that one is exposed to more promises in the new covenant. God promised Abraham in Gen. 17:1-2 that if he were to walk before Him and be blameless, He would establish His covenant and multiply him exceedingly. God also promises in Gen 12:2 to make Abraham a great nation and bless him to the extent that he would also be a blessing to others. God blesses us so that we can also bless others. Being linked with Jesus also connects you with the Abrahamic covenant and much more.

"Those who are of faith are blessed with Abraham, the believer" (Gal. 3:9).

The first covenant needed to be rectified because the children of Israel still continued in their sins. God decided to send His Son, Jesus to die for our sins, so that as many as believe in Him could receive the Holy Spirit who would help man live godly. It's not by might nor by power that one overcomes sin, but rather by the Spirit of God (Zech. 4:6). God wanted a new covenant in which man would naturally serve God from his heart, and not try to follow a set of rules or commandments. If man's heart could be changed through the operations of the Holy Spirit, then he would willingly and certainly want to do God's will.

"Behold the days are coming, declares the LORD,' when I will make a new covenant with the house of Israel and with the house of Judah, not like the covenant which I made with their fathers in the day I took them by the hand to bring them out of the land of Egypt, my covenant which they broke, although I was a husband to them, declares the LORD" (Jer. 31:31- 32).

The Children of Israel could not keep the law of God, because they needed a change of heart.

"I will put my law within them, on their hearts I will write it; I will be their God, and they shall be my people. And they shall not teach them again...for they shall all know me, from the least of them to the greatest of them" (Jer.31:32-34).

When the Holy Spirit takes over your life, a spiritual operation takes place whereby our spirits become receptive and follow the instructions and leadership of the Holy Spirit. God doesn't force or intimidate you into joining. It's not a kingdom one enters by killing others or through violence. God gently chides, *"See I have set before you today life and prosperity and death and adversity" (Deut. 30:15).* He advises us to choose life that we may live (Deut. 30:19).

When you believe that Jesus Christ died for your sins and that He rose again from the dead for your justification, opening up your heart to receive the Spirit of Christ (The Holy Ghost), you are born of the Spirit. The Holy Spirit speaks to your heart in a still, small voice encouraging you to eschew evil and perform the works of God. I like the way 1 Cor. 11 puts it,

"...but you were washed, but you were sanctified, but you were justified in the name of the Lord Jesus, and in the Spirit of our God"

With Jesus you can overcome any situation every day. God has given us a new covenant. He has given us a cup of breakthrough which is poured out with the new covenant in the blood of Jesus. (Luke 22:20). We don't have to struggle to live according to His will. His Holy Spirit is always there to direct and to guide us. With Jesus, you are always a winner.

CHAPTER 4
YOU CAN BE MADE RICH BY THE BLOOD

A Part of the package that comes with the blood is evidential fruitfulness or undeniable proofs of God's grace in your life. There is no glory in serving God and being unable to pay your bills or feed your family. That is why the Bible explains that Jesus died poor so that you might be rich.

"For you know the grace of our Lord Jesus Christ, that though He was rich, yet for your sake He became poor, that you through His poverty might become rich" (2Cor. 8:9).

Jesus left His throne, majesty and splendour in heaven to live an ordinary life in the flesh so that you and I could enjoy a life of prosperity. So happy am I that I gave my life to Christ quite early in life. I graduated as a Medical Doctor by the age of 24. By the time I was 25 years I had bought my first car (Benz). By the age of 38, I had obtained my PhD from a UK University. All these were achieved simply by following spiritual principles packaged in the blood.

Many people chase after worldly possessions, having anxiety neurosis and nervous breakdown, thinking of how they are going to get the latest clothes of the flashiest cars. Some have even developed hypertension hassling themselves about these issues. They chase worldly possessions and forget the One that gives blessings. They chase the blessing, boasting that they are 'self-made' and forget the *'Blessor'*. However, the Bible says we should not forget the LORD for it is He that gives us the power to get wealth (Deut. 8:18). It is not by labour but rather divine favour that one prospers. A sister told me she could feel objects moving all over her body with subsequent "internal heat". This is what is called a psychosomatic illness. This means that due to worry and anxiety, she actually starts experiencing physical symptoms. She had been worrying about where she would get money to pay her children's school fees. I advised her to get her mind and spirit back to God. We covered her in the blood of Jesus, claiming His healing power, and asked God to provide.

Jesus died poor that we may be made rich. The next time I saw her she had a smile on her face. Every form of depression had gone. She had been healed of her illness and yes! With hard work and prayers, God had been able to give her an idea that took care of her financial difficulties. God is far smarter than us. He advises that we should,

"seek first the kingdom of God and His righteousness and all these other things shall be added to you" (Luke 12:30).

Another sister developed hypertension as she didn't like her current job. By putting her problem in God's hand, and entreating the power of the blood, together with exercise and relaxation, her blood pressure came down to normal. She didn't get a new job, but she got to like where she had been deployed. Little did she realize that God had placed a marvelous surprise for her. Within a year, she was given a company car and the keys of a house as a form of incentive to stay with the company.

In Luke 12:22, Jesus advises us not to,

"worry about the food you need to stay alive, or about the clothes you need for your body. Life is more important than clothes".

The Apostle Peter advises us to cast all our cares on the Lord 1 Peter 5:7). God wants to bless you, but for this to come about, you have to follow the spiritual principle of seeking first the kingdom of God. Then all the other things such as goodness and mercy will begin to follow you supernaturally (Ps 23). If you seek after blessings, they will develop wings and fly away (Prov. 23:5). After you accept Jesus as Lord of your life, walk in His righteousness you become qualified for His blessings.

Some people are plagued with **"near success" or "merry-go-round syndrome".** When other people are getting contracts they are also notified, but when it comes to their own turn, however some misfortune happens/occurs and they are unable to get their breakthrough. They would be told "Aaah! If only you had come a bit earlier" or "if only you had come yesterday" you would have gotten the contract/job. The blood of Jesus destroys this near success syndrome when you follow the spiritual principle of sowing and reaping.

SOWING AND REAPING

The Bible says that sowing and reaping will never cease, as the earth exists (Gal. 6:7). In order to receive from God, you have to sow into His kingdom. That is, you have to give money for His work and for the furtherance of His gospel.

"Make for yourselves purses, which do not wear out, an unfailing treasure in heaven, where no thief comes near, nor

moth destroys. For where your treasure is there you heart will be also" (Luke 12:33-34)

You will notice that if you have no money in the stock market, you find you don't care whether the markets go up or down. However, the moment you start investing in the stock market, your heart begins to check the news as to whether your investments are going up or down. Where your treasure is, there will your heart be also. When Jesus was crucified on the cross of Calvary, His hands were pierced, so that your hands will never suffer lack.

When you sow into God's kingdom, your heart and mind is set on that kingdom and opens the bank of heaven for you to withdraw from. In Africa, you can buy crayfish at the local market. A good measure of small fish is placed in a metal container until it is full. The fish trader would then press the fishes down into the container so that some space is left on top of the container for more fish to be added until it overflows. This is how God wants to bless you, unto overflowing.

It is not just enough to empty all your finances into God's work and fold your arms. Sometimes God may work miraculously, but more often than not; you have to wait on the Holy Spirit to give you an inspired idea on how to get your breakthrough.

The Holy Spirit speaks to you in your heart, through the word of God (the Bible), or through an audible voice. For more information on the activities of the Holy Spirit, you can read my first book *"The Holy Ghost Revelation"*.

The Holy Spirit would give you the business acumen you need and lead you in making the right decisions in business. Jesus has paid the price for you. All you need to do is to walk in the confidence that God has taken over your finances. When you go to your work place in the morning ensure you cover the place in the blood of Jesus, asking for God's favour and direction throughout the day.

It is also very important to give your tithe to the work of God. Your tithe is one-tenth of your wages or salary. When you do this, you are telling Him to take control of your finances. God then gives you the wisdom to manage the remaining 90%. He promises that if you do this, he would open for you the windows of heaven, and pour out for you a blessing until it overflows. He also promises to rebuke the devourer (i.e. the devil) for your sake so that he does not destroy the fruits of your labour (Mal. 3:10-11). I believe that everybody pays tithes.

You either pay to God willingly, or reluctantly more to the devil in form of troubles, sicknesses and financial misfortunes. I prefer to pay to God and reap His blessings. When you pay your tithe, your finances will never be tight. As you follow God's biblical principles and cover every business transaction with the blood of Jesus, God is going to give you an overflowing, overthrowing financial breakthrough in Jesus' name.

CHAPTER 5
OVERCOMING POWER IN
THE BLOOD

I n the book of Revelations 12:11, we understand that there was a war in heaven. The angels of God were fighting with the demons of the devil. There was no breakthrough. There was an impasse. That is there was a stalemate. The angels of God then brought in the blood of Jesus. The Bible declares that:

"They overcame them (i.e. the devil and his cohorts) by the blood of the lamb and the words of their testimony"(Rev.12:11).

There is overcoming power in the blood of Jesus our testimonies from God's Word. There's a story of a hen that was caught in a raze of fire in a field. The fire burnt through the grasses and leaves of the field. The heat was intense. The little chicks of the hen tried in vain to escape. In a loving act of sacrifice, the hen gathered all the chicks together under her wings and shielded them from the heat of the fire. The fire scorched the fowl, but could not reach the little chicks. As the fire continued smolder, it seethed through the fowl forming blisters. The fowl's blood was shed and protected the chicks from the effect of the fire.

That is what the blood of Jesus does for you. Jesus died so that His blood could shield you from every work of darkness.

"No weapon formed against you shall prosper"

(Is. 54:17).

Small wonder the Bible says that though you walk through the fire you shall not be burnt (Is. 43:2). You need to have a personal conviction in these truths. It's not the quantity of scriptures that you know that will bring you breakthrough, but rather the level of your conviction and persuasion in the scriptures you know. You need to combine the working of the blood with the word of God. (i.e. the words your testimony). If for example you invoke prospering power in the blood concerning your finances, but continue to pronounce that you are poor and nothing is working for you, automatically you negate the earlier prayer.

The blood has to be mixed with the water of the word. In John 19:34, when Jesus was pierced after He died, water and blood were shed. (Naturally, the blood was supposed to have clotted). This was to signify the bond between the blood and the word of God. The Word of God as to be mixed with faith to be effective and profitable to you (Heb. 4:2). You should take time to study God's word and hide them in your heart.

1 John 5:6 informs us that Jesus came by water and the blood. Ephesians 5:26 also enlightens us that the washing of the water with Word of God sanctifies the church. In other words, the word of God, which is represented by water makes us clean. In John 15:3, Jesus also confirms that we are made clean by the word of God which is exalted above all His name (Ps 138:2). The blood is the oil that allows the wheels of the word to turn and give your

life a breakthrough. When you call upon the power in the blood of Jesus, the devil is unable to hinder you. In the book of Job 1:6 the devil is seen presenting himself to God and accusing Job. He is also described as the accuser of the brethren (Rev. 12:10). Job did not have the power of the Blood of Jesus to draw on. He ever cried about his need for a redeemer and a mediator (Job 9:33 19:25-27). Prophetically, He was referring to Jesus. As a result o the Power in the Blood of Jesus, the devil has been cast down from heaven.

The devil cannot accuse you of any unrighteousness, because you are covered in the blood of Jesus. In the court of heaven with Jesus as your solicitor, advocate and intercessor. The blood i your witness. It does not speak condemnation but rather i speaks redemption and salvation. The Blood of Jesus speak better things than the blood of Abel. No matter what sin you may commit, the moment you confess it to God and forsake it the blood of Jesus cleanses you from all sin.

"If we say we have no sin, we are deceiving ourselves and th truth is not in us. If we confess our sins, He is faithful and jus to forgive us and cleanse us from all unrighteousness" (1 Jn 1:8 9).

We don't need to live in guilt and defeat when we fall. Bu rather stand up and continue in the good fight of faith. Ther are times that the enemy the devil would like to remind you o sins that you have committed, causing you to confess the same sin many times due to guilt feeling. We can enter God's presence boldly because of the blood of Jesus.

"let us draw near with a sincere heart in full assurance of faith, having our hearts sprinkled clean from an evil conscience and our bodies washed with pure water" (Heb. 10:22)

USING THE BLOOD OF JESUS IN BATTLE

2 Cor. 10:3-4 enlightens us on the fact that *"the weapons of our warfare are not carnal, but mighty through God to the pulling down of strongholds, casting down imaginations and everything that exalts itself against the knowledge of God and bringing into captivity every thought to the obedience of Christ"*

One may ask what we need spiritual weapons for when we face physical circumstances every day. We need spiritual weapons because we are facing spiritual foes who are invisible and as such, that cannot be seen with the physical eyes. The things that are seen are actually temporal. The things that are not seen are eternal (2 Cor 4:18). We wrestle not against flesh and blood (i.e. physical human beings), but with spirits and demonic powers, which may use human agents. They have their chain of command. Ephesians 6:12, gives us insight on their hierarchy. They are divided into principalities, powers, rulers of darkness of this world, and spiritual wickedness in high places in descending order.

The devil uses all these forces to try to tie us down and stop us from fulfilling our God-given destiny. However, if God be for us, no one can be against us (Rom 8:31). The events, which occur in the spirit realm, control that of the physical realm. The first manuscript for this book got missing, but I had to persevere to ensure that it was rewritten and produced. All things work together for our good (Rom. 8:28). I was able to get more ideas and inspiration from God. The blood is one of the most potent weapons in the itinerary of the believer. It is to be used in concert with other weapons. The offensive weapons are important as the defensive weapons. There is a Scottish Tennis champion that was always being beaten by his Spanish counterpart. This was until he stopped playing defensively and started playing a more offensive style of play. Below are some weapons in the arsenal of the believer:

OFFENSIVE WEAPONS

a) The sword of the spirit (The word of God).

The word of God is hidden in the heart and pulled out to give lacerations, cuts and slits to the devil and his cohorts. That is why it is important to take time to study God's word. (Eph. 6:17). When Jesus was tempted by the devil, he kept repeating *"It is written...."* against the enemy until he fled from him (Matt. 4).

b) Praying in the spirit (Eph. 6:18).

We need to take the time to pray according to the leadership of the Holy Spirit, both in the understanding and in other tongues. Praying in tongues, we pray according to the perfect will of God (Rom 8:26). We also pray in the Spirit in the understanding, when we surrender our wills to the LORD and pray as led by the Spirit instead of our fleshly desires.

DEFENSIVE WEAPONS

a) The shield of faith (Eph.6:16).

This is used in quenching every dart of sickness, discouragement and destruction of the devil. Every weapon framed against you will be reversed back to the sender in Jesus' name. Faith is the key for your breakthrough. Faith in God. Faith in the ability given to you by God. Faith that no matter what you are going through, God is always in control and will see you through it successfully. You need the God kind of faith. This faith comes by hearing and hearing by the Word of God (Rom 10:17).

b) The helmet of salvation (Eph 6:17).

You need to be saved by making Jesus the Lord of your life. You need to believe that He died on the cross of Calvary for your sins and receive Him into your life as your Lord and personal Saviour. The Bible lets us know that with the heart, man believes unto righteousness and with the mouth confession is made unto salvation (Romans 10:10). This protects your head from the arrows of the devil and his agents. For a simple prayer to give your life to Christ, kindly pray the prayer in the last paragraph of Chapter 1 of this book.

c) The breastplate of righteousness (Eph 6:14).

You need to walk in the righteousness of God. Walking in holiness gives you power and confidence to face the enemy. A man with skeletons in his cupboard, is always fearful and never at ease. The righteous however is as bold as a lion (Prov. 28:1). The devil has no legal right to afflict a believer who is walking in the righteousness of God. Living in sin opens a hedge through with the devil may bite (Eccl. 10:8). As a child of God, you the righteousness of God in Christ Jesus (2 Cor. 5:21).

You are righteous not because of your works but because of your walk with God. You are righteous because of faith in Jesus Christ (Rom 3:22). Old things are passed away and all things have become new as the righteousness of Jesus is imputed on you as a gift by faith (Romans 4:13, 5:17). As the breastplate protects the heart of the soldier, holiness protects your heart and life from contamination of the enemy.

d) The belt of truth (Eph 6:14)

You need to walk in truth and integrity. This will keep you through all your endeavors. The belt strengthens you just the same way weight lifters tie belts around their waits to improve heir performance. Choose to walk in the truth of the Word of God. God's Word is Truth (John 17:17).

e) Shoes that spread the gospel of truth Eph 6:15)

We need to have our feet shod with the preparation of the gospel of peace. This means that we have to be ready and prepared to share the gospel of Jesus Christ. When you share the gospel in an environment, you find out that you always try to live up to the high standard that people expect of you. When you proclaim Jesus publicly and unashamedly, God will also ensure your life is acclaimed.

There are evil forces of darkness that use interested people in form of witches, wizards and agents of darkness to perpetuate their plans. Is it not wonderful to be under the protective power of the blood of Jesus?

THE BLOOD SHIELD

Isaiah 54:17 declares that no weapon formed against you shall prosper. When you are in Christ, you are covered in a shield with the blood of Jesus. As the mountains are all about Jerusalem, so does the LORD surround His people. There was a brother who was travelling in a minibus. As his vehicle was about to cross a narrow bridge, suddenly he noticed a trailer moving with high speed from the opposite direction. A head on collision was imminent or one of the vehicles would have to plunge into the river below, in desperation but with faith he called on the blood of Jesus. Inexplicably the two vehicles were able to pass thorough the bridge simultaneously with no accident taking place.

You need to cover yourself and your family in the blood of Jesus daily. The devil has no power when you are covered in the blood. In the book of Exodus when the angel of death ravaged the land of Egypt. The Lord commanded the children of Israel to kill unblemished lambs. He instructed them to sprinkle the blood on their doors (Ex.12:5). As many doorposts that were covered with the blood of the lambs would be passed over by the angel of death and their inhabitants would not be hurt. The firstborn children of the Egyptians were however plundered to death by the angel. The blood shield or bloodline shields its possessor from accidents sickness and every form of tragedy. Small wonder the Bible says that as the mountains are all about Jerusalem so does the Lord surrounds His people (Psalm 125:2) Remain shielded in the blood in Jesus name.

There is a story of a man whose farm was being ravaged by some evil foxes. He proceeded to plead a blood line of the Blood of Jesus around his farm. The next morning there were dead evil foxes around his farm. At some time, I was praying and pleading the blood line around my house, commanding every evil bird to be destroyed. The next morning, there was a dead bird in front of the house. By the power in the Blood of Jesus, I pray that every evil animal attacking your destiny be destroyed by fire and the Lion of the tribe of Judah in Jesus Name.

CHAPTER 6
PRAYING WITH THE BLOOD

A s we've seen in previous chapters, the blood is a powerful weapon that could be used in the spiritual realm either as a defensive weapon or as an aggressive spiritual bomb. There are many Christian who ignorantly have been walking in curses placed on them either through the sins of their forefathers or by spells cast on them by agents of darkness. When Jesus died on the cross of Calvary He destroyed every curse.

"Christ redeemed us from the curse of the Law, having become a curse for us-for it is written: 'cursed is everyone who hangs on a tree'- in order that in Christ Jesus the blessing of Abraham might come to the Gentiles, so that we might receive the promise of the spirit through faith" (Gal. 3:13-14).

Ancestral Curses

Ancestral curses are curses that are brought along a particular family line as a result, of sins one's ancestors or forefathers might have committed. Some individuals are walking in ancestral curses because some of their forefathers did some fetish practices in their days. Some families are plagued with some kinds of illnesses such as psychiatric or cardiovascular diseases. Some families are unable to prosper financially while others are highly immoral. Praise God because the blood of Jesus breaks every such curse.

When it comes to ancestral curses some basic steps should be taken to break them. You have to confess all known sins of your forefathers (such as human sacrifices) and ask God for His forgiveness and cleansing. Ask God to separate you from the sins of your forefathers. Reject every covenant with the devil and command all demons sent to your life and family to flee in Jesus name. Use the blood of Jesus to break every ancestral curse in Jesus name.

Incantation Curses

These are curses pronounced on people by those that they have wronged. Life and death are in the power of the tongue (Prov. 18:21). When people are cursed because of evil they have done, the curses may come to pass. Some people out of envy would try to curse others for no reason. These curses however cannot stand.

"The curse causeless shall not come" (Prov. 26:2).

Every incantational curse against your destiny is quenched and reversed by the Blood of Jesus in Jesus Name.

Witchcraft Curses

The agents of darkness may also try to put curses on those that they hate for no apparent reason. The heart of man could be desperately wicked. Be encouraged in the fact that as long as you are covered in the blood of Jesus and don't break the hedge no weapon formed against you shall prosper. Jesus in you is greater than he that is in the world. Every Witcraft and occultic curse against your destiny is destroyed in Jesus name.

Situational Curses

Some individuals enter situational curses by entering into cults or making blood covenants with agents of the devil. Such covenants have to be broken or the individual would continue struggling in life with no success.

I pray that every self -sabotage curse and curses as a result of broken covenants with the devil are broken in Jesus Name by the Blood of Jesus. You can walk out on the devil by the Blood of Jesus.

You have been redeemed by the Blood of Jesus

One of my brothers was taking care of a bookshop, when a wrinkled craggy old lady came into the shop in the guise of wanting to buy some books. As she walked round the shop my brother noticed that she was mumbling some words to herself. When he saw that she was not making attempt to buy a book he asked her what exactly she wanted. In reply she asked "what church do you attend?".

She had tried to place a spell on the bookshop with the aim of stealing some books and possibly some money. She had been involved in the activity for quite some time and was surprised to meet a stumbling block.

My brother talked to her about getting bigger and better power through the blood of Jesus. She gave her life to Christ, renounced the devil and has since been living for Christ with evidential fruitfulness. Jesus has broken every curse of the law and we are set free. Halleluiah!

"Christ redeemed us from the curse of the Law, having become a curse for us for it is written 'cursed is everyone who hangs on a tree' in order that in Christ Jesus the blessing of Abraham might come to the Gentiles, so that we might receive the promise of the spirit through faith" (Gal 3:13-14).

Below is a general prayer you can pray using the blood of Jesus. It can be tailored to your peculiar situation:

Father, I thank you for your grace upon my life. I pray that the glory of the LORD rests upon my life. People will see the glory of God upon my life. As a result of which, I shall eat the wealth of the nations and the riches of the gentiles. I pray that no weapon formed against me shall prosper and every tongue that rises against me in judgement shall be condemned. I pray that you prosper me abundantly, physically, spiritually, financially, materially and martially in Jesus name, amen.

Father I'm the one that serves you with my spirit, my soul and my body. Renew therefore thy glorious power within me, getting my inner man born again and to be stronger than all wicked spirits in the heavenly places, so that I shall run and not be weary and I will walk and not faint.

Father, I thank you for lightening my candle and getting me to be born again. I pray that you continue to enlighten my form of darkness in my life, now and forever more, Amen. Father you are my shepherd and I'm your sheep. I hear your voice and I follow you. The voice of strangers 1 will not hear and I will not follow.

I believe in the Bread of Life, the Lord Jesus Christ. By his confession, I use the blood of Jesus to cover my spirit soul and body. I use the blood of Jesus right now to destroy every single covenant that I might have with failure, poverty, setbacks, stagnation, financial limitations, promise and fail, non-achievements and near success syndrome, merry go round syndrome, rejection, depression, oppression, obsession, possession and every works of the flesh and darkness in Jesus Name.

I am of God and therefore I overcome Satan himself. This is because; greater is He that is in me than he that is in the world. I use the blood of Jesus to break every curse placed upon me by Satan and his agents. This is because the word of God declares that Jesus Christ has redeemed me from every curse of the law that the blessing of Abraham would come upon my life, that I might receive the Holy Spirit by faith. I use the blood of Jesus and I break free from every jinx, vex, voodoo, juju, charm, invocation, incantation, libation, spell placed upon me by any man woman, witch, or any wizard. I break the spells of hardship, separation, divorce, disappointment, failure, shame, hatred, barrenness, untimely death, poverty, demonic manipulations and evil dreams (eating, running or making love in the dream).

I thank you for you said in your Word, that surely, they shall gather but as many as will rise up against me shall fall for my sakes. As many as rise up against me shall be defeated before my face. Though they come one way, they will flee seven ways in Jesus Name. I pray that wherever they have gathered, are gathering or will gather. In the land, seas, air, tree, graveyard, witchcraft coven, the occult, herbalist home, junction, beach, marine kingdom, celestial kingdom, terrestrial kingdom. I say wherever they are calling my name for evil, I release, the Blood of Jesus against them in Jesus Name. I release Holy Ghost FIRE in Jesus name.

I use the blood of Jesus and I destroy spiritual husbands, spiritual wives, marine spirits and mermaid spirits. I destroy all the evil plans of the enemy by the blood of Jesus. I raise the standard of the blood of Jesus against principalities, powers and spiritual wickedness in high places, rulers of darkness of this word. I use the blood of Jesus and paralyses agents of darkness. I use the blood of Jesus to lock up all their transport routes in heavenly places.

I use the blood to destroy all their communication gadgets. I declare confusion and disunity in the camp of the enemy. I lock up the astral planes and frustrate the plans of witches and wizards. I release the bloodstone to pull down every goliath in my life. I release the bomb of the blood of

Jesus in the coven of agents of darkness and pronounce their destruction in Jesus name. Amen.

Thank you, Father, for the liberty that I have in the blood of your Son Jesus. Let your name be glorified in my life in Jesus' name Amen.

CHAPTER 7
THE HOLY COMMUNION

T he term Holy Communion denotes a sanctified state of being bound together in mutual love, confidence and fellowship with the Spirit of Jesus Christ. God has always wanted intimate fellowship with man. When Solomon was building the temple of God, he wondered if God could indeed dwell in a temple built by man.

"But will God indeed dwell with mankind on the earth. Behold the heaven and the highest heaven cannot contain thee; how much less this house which I have built" (2 Chron. 6:18).

Even the Psalmist could not fathom why God was so interested in man. God however wants to be close with His children just as we love our earthly children:

"What is man, that Thou dost take thought of him? And the son of man that Thou dost care for him? Yet thou hast made him a little lower than God and dost crown him with glory and Majesty!" (Ps. 8:4-5).

When Jesus died on the cross of Calvary, the curtain covering the Holy of Holies where God communed with the priests was torn in two, signifying that God was no longer confined to the temple, but rather, His Spirit could enter the hearts of as many as received Him.

"Moreover, I will give you a new heart and put a new spirit within you; and I will remove the heart of stone from your flesh and give you a heart of flesh. And I will put my Spirit within you and cause you to walk in My statutes, and you will be careful to observe them" (Ez. 36:26).

We don't have to struggle to live righteously. We just need to open our hearts and commune with God's Spirit. He will guide us and lead us by convicting our spirits on how to live according to God's will.

Before Jesus was crucified he gathered His disciples for His last supper during the Passover ceremony. He sat with His twelve disciples that night by the wooden dining table as he began to give His farewell speech. He promulgated the sacrament of the Holy Communion to signify the work that He did on the cross. He commanded that we should perform it as often as possible so that we can mediate on how He saved mankind and reconciled us back to God.

"And when he had taken some bread and given thanks He broke it and gave it to them saying 'This is my body which is given for you; do this in remembrance of Me.' And in the same way He took the cup after they had eaten, saying 'This cup which is poured for you is the new covenant in My blood' (Luke 22:19-20)".

The Holy Communion is the key to walking in God's favour and blessings in the new covenant.

"Is not the cup of blessing which we bless a sharing in the blood of Christ"? (1 Cor. 10:16)

When you walk with God you are always a winner. The mystery of the Holy Communion is a physical replica of the fellowship we are to have with God through the death and resurrection of His Son Jesus Christ. You need the Holy Spirit in your life. Jesus told his disciples that they shall receive Power after the Holy Ghost has come upon them. (Acts 1:8). This was evident in Acts 2, when they were seen boldly declaring the gospel and God's glory. You need the Holy Spirit to advise you in business decisions, relationships and even academics. I've gone to many examinations where I knew the questions that were going to come out before they did. Some of my colleagues started consulting me to tell them which questions were likely to come out in our exams. Take time out to spend in God's Presence. In His Presence, there is fullness of Joy and at his right Hand are pleasures for ever more (Ps 16:11).

We need the Holy Spirit to help us to pray. We need Him to direct us on which area of our lives or others, we should concentrate on in prayers. Spending time in God's presence through prayers. Praising and worshipping Him opens you up to wonderful fellowship and blessings. I always notice God's Presence powerfully in my room when I spend time to praise and worship Him. This is because He inhabits the praises of His People (Ps 22.3).

''And in the same way, the Spirit also helps our weakness; for we do not know how to pray as we should, but he Spirit Himself intercedes for us with groanings too deep for words'' (Rom 8:26).

There are times you may want to go out or travel and the Holy Spirit will gently chide to your spirit that you should not go out, in order to prevent some tragedy. I was in a plane travelling from the United Kingdom to Boston USA for holiday, when I was upgraded to first class (as my video panel was not working). After some hours enjoying the first-class service, I was led in my spirit to go back to economy class. With difficulty, I obeyed and returned. As soon as I returned the video panel started working. As the plane landed, it skidded moving from side to side before landing safely with all the passengers giving a sigh of relief and a round of applause. I believe obeying the Holy Spirit averted tragedy from taking place.

We need God's fellowship. Our bodies are now living temples of God in which the Holy Spirit dwells (1 Cor 6:19). We are hence enjoined to forsake any form of immorality and live holy lives for Jesus. Have a wonderful time of fellowship with the Holy Spirit in Jesus Name. As many as are led by the Spirit of God are indeed the sons of God (Rom 8:14).

"The grace of the Lord Jesus Christ, and the love of God, and the fellowship (communion) of the Holy Spirit, be with you all" (2 cor. 13:14) Amen.

CHAPTER 8
THE HEALING POWER IN THE BLOOD

P art of the packages in the blood covenant is that of healing. To be healed means to be made whole, to be set free from every sort of infirmity. Jesus was smitten on the cross of Calvary so that you may not be smitten by any sickness of affliction.

There was a lady who was admitted in a hospital. She had hypertensive disease in pregnancy. She had six other pregnancies in the past. Whenever she gets to the seventh month, the pregnancy would abort and she would have a miscarriage. As I ministered to her, led her to Christ and told her to place her condition in God's Hands.

We called on God and covered her pregnancy with the blood of Jesus. We stood on God's word, which says that she shall deliver like the Hebrew woman (Who delivers quickly with no pains or complications). I also gave her some anointing oil to use in faith. Soon after that, she went into labour and had precipitated delivery of a bouncing baby boy after six miscarriages. To God be the glory. Her hypertensive disease also subsided after the delivery.

All your sicknesses and diseases were laid on Jesus when He died on the cross. You don't have to carry any burden from the devil. See Jesus carrying that physical ailment disturbing you. I

He is carrying them, then you should be free. Have faith in God's word and the power in the blood of Jesus.

"Surely our griefs He himself bore, and our sorrows. He carried; yet we ourselves esteemed Him stricken, smitten of God and afflicted. But He was pierced through for our transgressions He was crushed through for our iniquities; the chastening for our well-being fell upon Him, and by His scourging (stripes), we are healed" (Is. 53:4-5).

Even when you still feel symptoms of illnesses continually affirm that Jesus has died for every sickness and that by His stripes, you are healed. All the scourging Jesus received was for your healing. The basic ingredient needed is faith. Have faith in God. Have faith in the power of the blood. Jesus spent three years of His life healing people who were oppressed with sickness (Acts 10:38). This shows how much He desires your healing.

"Beloved, I wish above all else that you may prosper and be in good health, just as your soul prospers" (3 Jn. 1:2).

There are over 50 scriptures on healing in the Bible. In Jeremiah 17:14, the prophet declares, *"heal me O LORD and I shall be healed".* He knew all he had to do was to believe.

Apart from accepting God's word on healing, we also need to take steps to prevent ourselves from acquiring disease. There is a man of God I know who declared boldly during one of his sermons that he can't remember when last he fell ill. I went to visit him at his house and could see why this was so. The whole house was sparkling clean. The room was air-conditioned and hence not conducive for mosquitoes and other insects that cause disease in man.

The rugged evangelist John Wesley even commented, *"cleanliness is next to godliness".* We should ensure that we are clean and don't leave any room for micro-organisms to enter our bodies. We should eat responsibly and avoid food that predispose to hypertension and cardiovascular disease (Such as too much salt and saturated fats). We should take time to exercise.

Even the scriptures confirm, "bodily exercise gives little profits" (1 Tim. 4:8). We should go after the little profits that we can get. Some individuals cook some food and allow it to stay for days before eating it. They end up getting gastroenteritis. They should blame themselves and not the devil. We should eat our food soon after cooking and always remember to cover our food when we are not ready to eat. Simple techniques, such as washing one's hands before eating can help prevent many diseases. Always be enthusiastic about getting all the information you can about your health.

SPIRITUAL HEALING

The Blood of Jesus also provides healing for hurts to the soul and heart. As I was writing this section of the book, I felt a wave of depression trying to come over me for no apparent reason. Then I remembered that Jesus bears every form of grief and depression. So why should I be carrying one?

"Surely our griefs He Himself bore and our sorrows He carried" (Is. 53:5).

We are to see him carrying those things that get us down. If we can visualize this, it would make life much happier and easier for us. King David who had passed through rigorous times in his life advices us to put all our burdens and trepidations on the LORD. In 1 Peter 5 :7, the apostle Peter also urges us to cast all our cares on Jesus for He cares for us. It all depends on us to make up our minds to be happy.

"Cast your burden upon the LORD, and He shall sustain you. He will never allow the righteous to be shaken." (Ps. 55:22).

When someone has betrayed or offended you, don't allow the hurt of unforgiveness come over you. Quickly forgive and get it out of your heart. It's very easy for us to forgive others most especially at the times when we remember the hideous ways we've offended God. Yet He still forgives when we confess and forsake our sins. (1 Jn. 1:7).

The blood purges, purifies and washes you from every hurt of guilt. When we sin, the devil may try to weigh us down with guilt feelings. The blood of Jesus which speaks better things than the blood of Abel, speaks for your justification.

"But you have come to Mount Zion and to the city of the living God and to Jesus, the mediator of a new covenant and to the sprinkled blood, which speaks better things than the blood of Abel" (Heb. 12:22-24).

The blood of Jesus speaks redemption and deliverance. He sets you free from every spiritual hurt. You don't have to go through life crawling. You are a winner. You are more than a conqueror. Greater is God that is in you. God is lifting you up as an eternal Excellency and as a joy unto many generations.

"And not through the blood of goats and calves, but through His own blood, He entered the holy place once for all, having obtained eternal redemption. For if by the blood of goats and bulls and the ashes of a heifer sprinkling those who have been defiled, sanctify for the cleansing of the flesh, how much more will the blood of Christ, who through the eternal Spirit offered Himself without blemish to God, cleanse your conscience from dead works to serve the living God?" (Heb. 9:12-14).

The blood of Jesus cleanses you. So, you don't have to walk with a guilt feeling in your conscience. The devil knows you can only do God's work faithfully when you are happy and at rest. So, he'll try all he can to take away your peace. Thank God, that we have Jesus, the Prince of Peace in our hearts. When you call on the blood, an alarm rings in heaven and angels are placed at your disposal. Empowered by the blood, they would come to your aid.

SOME HEALING CAPSULES PROM THE WORD

"Come let us return to the LORD, for He has torn us, but He will heal us" (Hos. 6:1).

When we walk outside God's will, He 'ill prick our conscience, but this is to bring us unto repentance and forgiveness, not condemnation., He heals both our hearts and our body.

"The Spirit of the LORD is upon Me, because He anointed Me to preach the gospel to the poor. He has sent me to proclaim release to the captives and recovery of sight to the blind. To heal the broken hearted and proclaim the favorable year of the LORD" (Luke 4:18-19).

Jesus is anointed to still heal those who are broken hearted. No matter what is making you feel hurt in your heart, simply cast your burdens on Jesus.

"For I will restore you to health and I will heal you of your wounds[1] declares the LORD" (Jer. 30:17).

Receive your healing from God by faith in Jesus Name.

"I am the LORD that health thee" (Ex. 15:26).

God is still in the business of healing you.

"Bless the LORD O my soul who pardons all your iniquities; who heals all your diseases" (Ps. 103:1-3).

"He heals the broken hearted and binds up their wounds"
(Ps. 14 7:3).

"But for you who fear My name the sun of righteousness
will rise with healing in its wings'' (Mai. 4:2).

"I have seen his ways, but I will heal him" (Is. 57:18).

Even though we are not perfect, God still heals us when we are humble and have a contrite spirit

"He sent forth his word and healed them and save them
from their destruction" (Ps. 107:20).

God's word is available to heal you of any disease or affliction.

THE TOTAL PACKAGE

I believe that as you follow the spiritual principles outlined in this book, your life would be radically transformed. The weapons of our warfare are not carnal, but mighty through God to the pulling down of strongholds (2 Cor 10:3-4). Every stronghold in your life is pulled down today. Continue steadfast in prayer standing on God's word and waiting on the Holy Spirit to lead you on how to pray and walk in God's will. 1 pray God will take you to a higher and richer level in Christ in Jesus name Amen.

Write to us at holyghostchapeluk@yahoo.com

Visit our website at www.holyghostchapel.org

ABOUT THE AUTHOR

Dr Kingsley Oturu is a Medical Doctor, a graduate of University of Sokoto, Nigeria with a special calling to teach the Word of God. He has a diploma in expository preaching from Faith Mission Bible College, Edinburgh and a PhD in international Health from Queen Margaret University, Edinburgh, Scotland UK.

He is from a Christian home and gave His life to Christ while at King's College Lagos in 1989. He is a Public Health Specialist and works with a variety of educational and health institutions in the UK and globally.

He has a passion for helping the underprivileged and is a serial social entrepreneur setting up international charities (such as the African Scottish Development Organization- www.asdoonline.org.uk and the Holy Ghost Chapel- www.holyghostchapel.org).

He gives new insight and revelation that leads you to appreciate that you can overcome all circumstances by the Blood of Jesus.

Printed in Great Britain
by Amazon

76530862R00037